VOYAGE through EMOTIONS

Poems on Love, Humanity, Patriotism and More

SALEEM RAZA

ISBN 979-8-88815-683-4

To My Beloved Parents

Contents

Foreword

I am deeply honored to be writing this foreword for one of my favourite writers and artists, in a first book that is truly a point of arrival in what has been—and what will continue to be—a remarkable and wonderfully creative and artistic journey.

Saleem Raza has been part of GloMag (a poetry and prose magazine that I edit and publish) almost since its inception, presenting his work in his own gentle and unobtrusive way. He sent in poetry at the beginning, but eventually I became aware that Saleem is a very talented artist too. This I found out by visiting his timeline and gazing—awestruck—at the paintings and sketches that he posted there. Amazing works! At some point, I approached him for a painting, for the cover of one of the monthly issues of GloMag, and he graciously complied. We, on GloMag, were so delighted with his work!

As time went by, he started sending in prose pieces as well that were thought-provoking and interesting. Throughout this time, he was also holding a full-time job and living away from his family. His creativity seems to weave into the fabric of his life, lighting up and brightening his world and ours. It is not easy to hold a full-time job and yet be persistently and determinedly creative. This speaks volumes about his commitment and discipline.

In this collection, it is hard to pinpoint a theme, a common thread that connects all these poems, except for the poet, his moods, his insightful thoughts…his musings if you will… Thus, each poem should be read individually, for its own message and for the way it is presented.

Sometimes, it's these experiences…times when the Human Spirit overcomes adversaries, sometimes, it is philosophical musings and

Infinite ways of saying 'I love you':

A dig at the arrogance and entitlement with which human beings take their surroundings and other species and Nature for granted.

Many more poems thoughts! A very interesting collection indeed! I am sure that this first book is just the beginning of a very exciting journey, and I wish Saleem Raza all the very best in all his future endeavors.

– Glory Sasikala

(Editor and Publisher of GloMag)

After the flood

It was raining day and night;
an unknown fear
started to erupt.

For each hour
had it heavy shower.
Torrents continued
for many hours.
Swamps and drain overflew,
Streams, roads, and bridges
seemed like a roaring ocean.

Floodwater has shown
Its' face of wilderness.
It has broken the barricades,
and quickly risen as we look.

Muddy water from landslides
flown in high velocity

from highlands.
Dams opened without
proper measures.
Our homes and dreams
floated as vessels.

Though we have lost
our earnings the most,
our determination
and unity stood, to uphold
our slogan: Unity is the power.

Thus, we,
the people of this tiny land
delivered the message
to the entire nation,
that, no one can blast
our amalgamation.

But, after the great tragedy,
when I see a darkened sky,
it turns me into fear;
my mind slips to another gear.
When I see rain clouds
in the far horizons
an unknown pain ensues
in the depth of my soul.

When I hear
the sound of whistling air
murmuring with
the Western Ghats,
an absolute silence
spreads in the valley,
and the lushly lands.

Suddenly, it began
yet another rain
my shivering lips whispered
"Aye, madden clouds
drop not anymore.
We had enough and more."

Beautiful is night

Beautiful is night,
that's what inspires the
spirit of an optimist;
but not of a pessimist.

Beautiful is darkness
since the spheres of light
loosen its sharpness;
and when the buds of
our dreams blossoms
into happiness.

For you and me, my dear
could never see things clear,
though, the darkness of
the day meets the brightness of
the night, through
our silent, frozen eyes.

Because we are not witness
to the world of nastiness,
darkness is happiness.
Beautiful is night.

Beyond the time

With thousands of bloomed
cherry flowers in the eyes;
(those with white petals
and pink shades to be precised)
I have waited for you all the way;
from the moment, you've flown away.

Keeping me alone
you've floated away
as willows flowers moves away
in the wind, you've gone away
from the foliage of my mind.

Winter has come with its frozen wings
to cool up my mind
but it was boiling behind.
The aroma of spring was not
enough to equate the fragrance
of your presence.

The brightness of your face;
and glitters of your eyes
was much brighter than that of
a summer shine.

Autumn colors found as
faded gray, before your
splendid thoughts, and awesome acts.

Oh, my beloved;
no season could ever turn
my attention from the florescence
memories about you,
that is flaming in
the depth of my heart.

Broken memories

"Have you ever had dreams?"
(Once she asked.)
"… Yes." – I told.
"But my dreams!".
"Your dreams!?"
"Y eh, … I can't tell.".
"Why?"
"Because they have no languages;
I tried to paint it,
but I came to know that,
I can't find a colour palette
for my dreams.
I tried to remember its smell
but my dream was odorless."

"Then? …"
(She was curious, her eyebrows rose like a bow.)
"What was your dream about?"

after some moments: -
I told
"At last, I picked up some scattered
pieces of memories,
and linked them together"

(by nodding her head… mmmm…)

"Then found its language
was infinite and uncertain,
Its color was dusty and smoky.

It was smelled like the
soured sweats of a peasant;
It smelled like burning
stomach of a child;
menstrual bleed of a woman.

It was about faded,
candlelight-like paled women.
starving children;
about victims of a massacre,
frightened faces in a battlefield;
It was about…
struggling mankind;
the absolute common men.

"Yes! … You, you… have
Really had dreams…"
(She told).

But you

I was sure that time, somewhere
in the corridors of my life,
I'd fall in love with you;
that has happened.

I was sure that time,
that one day, you would
look at the wounds of my
weeping heart, that has happened.

I had never thought that,
in the midways, we would
be enforced to separate in two ways,
but that has happened.

I always had impulse thought
that, as if all the streams

do meet in ocean, we could
meet again, but that hasn't happened.

Now, I'm neither sure of anything
nor thinking of anything,
but you…

Black N White

Black:
A time will come for the people
to realize what you have
had in the depth of your heart.
Whether it was white
as you look from out,
or Is it as my outer look,
as others say 'black'

White:
May be I am black inside,
but the world look only at one side
And I am privileged by all the side.
 I'm being treated at first
in every stage; utmost.
Then, who cares what's inside?

But you could never be in my state
at least for another two decades,
it will continue to hesitate;
Though, in the depth of your heart is white.

I know, but my friend,
It's your fate to be sealed as it
In the shoddy perspective of this world.

Death living in the street

Heart-shaped leaves of
banyan trees, besides
the main streets, shivered
like the sword of oracles,
as they receive ashes
and smokes emerged from pyres,
where, the naked corpses
been buried.
It's in the street under the nose of
the so-called 'majesties'
but who cares!?

Mass cremations of victims
of the great pandemic has been
risen to the peak.
Echos of the hearse's sirens
hanged out in the air,

as if the cries of a fowl of death!,
but who hear!?

City streets seemed like
cemeteries, white uniformed
bodies laid randomly across
the streets, waited for their term.

Nature became wet because
of tears slumped from the eyes
of their dears.
City allies stand intense,
and fear, as carcasses floated
in the sacred rivers.

Shadow of fear reflected
in all faces, they screamed and
shouted for air to breathe;
But no one responded.
Instead, the uncivilized,
unsympathetic autocrats
threatened those innocents.

Mortals have increased
in hours, street graves piled up.
Carrion floated in
holy waters.

Gulmohar trees filled with
Red 'corona' flowers.
Cannibals cleared the path
to yet another business.
Leaves of Banyan trees trembled
in fear, as they witnesses
Deaths, living in the streets.

Glow of freedom

I looked at the plane of
freedom thru the eyes of
my ancestors.

Golden rays of happiness
have spread in all the faces of
those who lived that phases.

They had their rights
to chant slogans, even those
were opposing their leaders,
But, they were not
caught behind bars.

They read what they want to,
and they sipped their
morning coffee with a
strong blend of freedom;
and read true news in proud.

They wrote what they felt
because they were not
under a seal.
They ate their favorite meal;
and they engaged with a good deal.
They moved as free as
they wish, without fear of
gang rape and perish.
They were neither lynched
nor smash, because, there was
no question of what religion
or caste they belongs.

They grew up in a mixed culture,
mixed society, and with mixed thoughts;
but they kept lots of treasures of
freedom and love.
That for now, lost its meaning and glow.

Hidden things

I know that I have been
there before; but when?
or where?, I cannot tell.

I know the valley,
with a blanket of grass,
and a ripped little cherry
in its slopes.
But how sweet was it?
I could never say…

I know, that you have
also been there, but for
What? and when?
I am not able to say.

I have sipped the sweetened
red wine from your lips

and floated in the infinite
blue skies thru your eyes
but when? or how?
I may not know.

I know, that I have heard
the melodious song;
but from where? and why?
I can not tell.

I knew when we met at first
your body was made of love!
but by whom? and when?
I would never know.

I can only tell one thing
that, everything
happens in a divine way.

Hunger

They put cockroaches
into my food.
I posted them on
Facebook and on Instagram;
then it became viral!

They started to root out
a community, irradiate
the ruins of history! Instead,
erected new faces and statues.

I tried to bring it out
to the world, then they
have broken my food plate;
and imposed sanctions on me.

They put handcuffs on
my hand, and removed the

Ribbon, that was
tied around the eyes of
the Goddess of justice,
and fastened my mouth with that.
And they poured black oil
into the eyes of the
Goddess of justice.

After some while,
sitting on the peak of
a black day,
I have painfully tried
to raise my locked hands
and peacefully tried to chant
by my restrained mouth,
I was struggling to yell…
I'm hungry…I'm hungry;
hungry for freedom
" Azaadi"… "Azaadi"

In lieu of your love

What shall I return to you;
in lieu of your love?
Shall I offer you a rose?
or a bunch of roses?
oh, that's quite a cliche
and meant for youngsters
as remembrance of
their first day in falling love.

What shall I return
in lieu of your love?
Shall I offer you the streams?
As like as in the valleys of
Heaven, where milk and
honey always flowing thru?,

Oh, that's quite exaggerated
since I'm not a superstitious,

you would be looking
at me, thinking that
I'm mocking on you.

What shall return
in lieu of your love?
Shall I offer you my life?
believe me, some deep
lovers really do that!
Oh, now you might be thinking
What kind of life
do I have to offer?

After all,
Was it not a failure?
as my love to you?.

Not for him,... But

Things have changed
between dusk and dawn;
He became barely have
anything to lose.

As of those goons:
From now onwards,
his home is not for him,
neither his wife,
nor his children are!

The air he breathes, water he drinks,
the food he eats, and feed to
would never be again with him.

The land he stand
have already eyed by someone.
The sky and mountains he

sees daily, the river that flows
through his village, the nature
that always protected him
has some unknown claimant!

Its pity to say that,
all of sudden, he became
a stranger in his land,
a refugee in his country.
But all what he has is his willpower
to fight for his right,
till his last breath; and courage
to proclaim that, being
the son of this sacred land,
the citizen of this great country,
all its resources are belongs to him too;
And would never give up
nor compromise with a checkmate.

Let it be any colour, race and religion,
But, we are one.
Though, we speak different languages
it sounds like one, as we are one.

Nature of our love

We are sharing a special
kind of love,
that no other couple
can have like us;
Because,
We didn't fall in love
But,
we have grown in love.

I pray to the Almighty,
To let our love, be the
Enduring one.
Let it spread the
Fragrance of heaven,
Let it be the icon of
Being together
And, let us be together
Even in the paradise.

Promise on separation

Get me back the kisses
that you have taken on
credit from me,
on a misty and hazy night,
that I could never forget.

On that cool and rainy night;
you had an ardent
desire, and ceaseless thirst
for my love and pat.

Give me back the waves of
my love, before the shore of
your mind gets dried;
and change like a desert.

Get me back the blue lotus
I nurtured in your heart,

the red wine I brewed in your lips
after all, the tiny particles of
wicked life pulses in your womb,
that caused a typhoon
to blow in your mind;
the source of downpour
in your eyes;
return back to me.

Instead; (If you can)
you may detach
your soul from me,
and get the face mask
you have hide from me;
you may take off the fragrance
of your body from me,
to share it with the privacy
of your dreams;
I would never be there,
I promise.

(If you wish),
you may choose your way
expect me not,
neither a call, nor a back-call.
proceed till you succeed.

Do not say goodbye,
I would be looking at you
on all your way,
till you vanish away.

I promise; I would never, ever
be there, anyway.

Reminiscence

The wet evening is in
its last breath,
my beloved, sit beside and
watch the blood stains
splashed out from the
darkened rainy clouds.

The wet evening is in its last breath
my dear, let us sit together
for some time, in this balcony,
to witness the magic of nature,
to see the vanishing moment
of the unseen thread; that
separates the day and night,
to swear on the fall of night.

Beloved, be close to me,
thought, now it is not allowed to be

but it is quite a long,
since the last time we
have spent some lovely
moments; and let me
catch on some old memories,
those are shivering afar from
the blueish curtain of moonlight.

Hey darling,
I could feel your moist eyes.
The pain of losses may last
for years; but the glow of gains
Would stay only for a short span.

Y..eh, it's drizzling outside;
a mischievous wind has
spread seeds of chills around;
Together, let us dive
Into the pool of memories,
and pick up some
broken pieces of pearls
and corals of happiness.

Read, read in the name of...

You woke him up from
A state of meditation in
The cave of darkness;
In the era of superstition;
And asked him to read…

Read, in the name of the Lord;
Who has created you,
From a clinging drop of blood.
You gave him the sward
Of light, and he, lead
The universe to the elite;
At a time, when the
Entire society was fumbling
In darkened craters of ignorance.

His guidance showed us
Some brightened

Dawn of good hopes.
You have built a palace
For him, in your empire;
You loved him the most,
And he, who lit lamps of
Knowledge; so, the seeds of
Mercy and humanity
Have begun to spurt
Underneath, In the hearts
And thoughts of mankind.

Mankind,
Your most beautiful
Creatures; Among those,
It was he, who born with
Shining face, shined out like
The sun and moon In one,
As if a soul of light
Covered him like
A full moon night;
With the Milky way of
Shining stars on one side
And at the same time,
He looked as if a
Brilliant sunny day.
It was he, whom you
Created as a human being,

But he was not like
The other human beings,
But, a flawless diamond
Shining forever,
And the rest
Is just as like stones.

May God's blessings be
Upon him; and may it be
Upon us too…on the
Day of Judgment,
To protect us from
The mouth of roaring fire.

Stance of a lost love

Oh dear,
if you could hear
me a moment,
I shall sing a stance of love.

Green leaves of maples
have lost their hue,
to a golden glow,
as the rays of autumn sun
falls and reflects on your cheeks.

Sometimes,
the melancholy songs
played by flute;
that you have heard
in the lonely night
would be the weeps
of my broken heart.

Oh! dear,
if you were near,
we could have fled in the air
with colorful wings,
as we saw in our dreams;
that we've woven in
the days we spent together.

My dear,
come here,
maples are waiting
for the spring to welcome
you with its shoots.

Rainbow is shining
in the skies to glitter
your marvelous eyes.

I'm writing these lines
from the shore of
*Bosporus straits,
where Seagulls always
cries of sorrow with salty tears.
They fly up and down,
in search of their lost love.

My dear,

come beside,

though the sun is in

the last sigh, to set in

the depths of Bosporus strait.

Summer vacation

In the courtyards of
a past vacation
my beloved daughter,
I could see your footsteps
as if some soft petals
of little roses sprinkled
on the naked floors.

In the valleys of my mind,
your unclear words echoed
like the jingling sound of an anklet.

When you are beside me,
my love for you is like a cascade fall
that makes millions of
white water droplets
and fill the surroundings
with mist and moisture.

Hey, my little cuckoo,
there's only a sunset is left
to say bye to you,
though,
let me fill my pallet
with the colors of
a splendid vacation
and leave me again
to wave the dreams alone,
on the branch of
a yet another summer tree.

The departure

Oh, my little daughter,
you came in my dream
to bother me, of your departure.
Sending you alone,
that caused my heart's aperture.
On our way to the airport,
the only sound I heard
was my weeping heart beat.
The only seen in my eyes
was your faded little face,
and tearful eyes.

The broken slices of solace
scattered in the runways
was wet with tears.

When your flight
elevate to the infinite,

I had a look back to the fate
of being apart.

Though it was cloudy, somewhat
a lightning radiant
passed through the other part.

'Continue the journey', be in peace;
she would one day realize
that, it was for her bliss
and to live in
the realm of her choice.

The eternity

Oh! the eternal love,
what shall I call you?
oh! immortal beauty,
how do I compare you?
since everything is made of you,
as everything in you,
and you are in everything.

You left no space for others,
but no one knows the moment
how,when and where you've begun.
Though, I realize that,
you have neither had a beginning
nor have an end,
that's why you are eternal!.

The enduring beauty and eternity,
your love causes to the tranquility

for the entire universe,
galaxies and creatures.

You love and comfort
those who had abide you,
from all the perspectives.

You are the most compassionate
and the most merciful.
Your supremacy is unquestionable;
and you are the incomparable.

The victims of a hellish act

She laid down on a
mangled mat, alongside a
crowded street, in the most
happening city's heart.

She stayed looking at
everyone passing by,
to get some penny
for bread to buy.

Waving in the air,
with her twisted hands,
abnormally swollen head,
and two holes in the place
of ears, a tiny nose,
and popped eyes, but no lids.
Though she smiles,
that of quite an innocence.

Her mom sat beside;
wrinkled, paled, and abstained
from the rhythms and
memories of the past;
picked up coins with
memories of the cursed destiny
presented to her,
and the entire village,
by spraying the toxic
Pesticides, from atop
a fertile land of cashew crop,
caused to a ghastly mishap,
that would never cure
into a normal shape.

The rulers always keep
swindling us, with their
blown promises.

The victims of this drastic
tragedy would never bring
as what they were,
rather, many ominous
births would take place.

Corporate giants will look
for another network,

to make the air we breathe,
the water we drink
get remains tainted.

Mothers will feed toxic
breast milk to their babes,
we will continue to act
as if, nothing have heard or seen
and will keep in a painful silence.

By the time, the cannibal giants
would reach to our doorsteps……

The kindly light

Mother,
she makes everything nice
in all the beautiful ways.
Mother taught us how to love,
and to be loved, by
feeding us her breast with pride.

Mother,
she fills the pigments of love;
in all her life, and
kept it for ever to be alive
that gave us the hopes to live.

Mother,
when she holds us in her arms
we feel the utmost
protection from all harms
When she plants buds of

kisses in our cheeks
we get a garden of roses,
with her tender kisses in our hearts.

Mother,
she could never be alone or idle
but always in the middle
of her dears and nears.

Mother,
she is the cause of harmony
in our life, the cause of buds
to bloom, cuckoos to sing,
she is the cause of light in our home,
she is the kindly light.

The turning point

Open your eyes
and look at the dice,
before the leaders
play their game of
political cataracts,
and, pull us into the
frightening darkness.

Open your ears and
hear everything twice,
before the venomous
typhoon blows
from terrorist's factories
and monasteries.
If not, they could
spoil your eardrums.

Open your mouth
against the culprits,
fascists, and scammers;
from east to west and
north to south,
before the delirious and
devilish dance, they perform
with your tongue in their hands.

Keep your steps strongly,
(yes, it's your land)
and move along your way…
to the Isle of peace,
to live without fear,
before they shatter our
earth under your foot.

Move forward,
till reach to the valleys of
eternal love, where you
could sit and listen
the morning conch horns
from the sacred temples of
the great Himalayas,
the bells of peace rung from
the holy shrines of Bethlehem
and you Could hear

the chant of the uniqueness.
(There is none to adore, but God)
from the holy Ka'aba sheriff. …
Everything in one,…One in everything.

The White sands

Oh, the land of white sands,
and the emerald waters!
my heart collides when I hear
about the souring pain of your soul.

I can see how depth is
the wound, caused by throwing
the stump of hesitation into
the innocent minds.

Oh! glittering blue waves,
will your love for the
crystal reefs be in vain? and push
a realm to the non-healing pain?

Will the purity of white sands
caused by your kisses
be mixed with the poison of

religious fanaticism?
Oh! my sweet people of
the exquisite land,
Will your dreams collapse of
the devilish action of
the mud-filled minds?
Will your harmony break?
Will the colour of the sacred sand change?

I hope the clouds of terror and
the uncertainty would merge
and vanish in the depth of the whirlpools
then, you could see the coral reefs
shining again, and the radiant of
hope rising with the dawn.

There it happens everyday

In the paradise,
every day it happens;
sometimes, on the land too.

Married couple,
who lived here with
trust and love for each other,
may extend their life in paradise.

Lovers,
who have faith in each other,
would meet in heaven,
to live together.

For someone,
on earth, if they were apart
they may get only a single berth
in the promised land to tolerate.

In the paradise every day it happens
sometimes on this land too.

Elderly men and women,
who lived on earth,
with passion for life and love,
would live forever in eternal love.
even though, they haven't
had enjoyment on earth.

Children who lost life
between lips and nipple
would get their mom
to be loved and feed.

In heaven, love happens always
sometimes on earth too

In heaven,
everything happens at its best,
to the supernatural crest
but on earth,
it's quite below the zest.

But, you and I could make
our earth heavenly, as heaven.

Fight against the
evils and egos residing
within me, and you;
and let the heavenly love
be on earth.
Then say
'Love happens always on earth too'.

Twins

We have born together
if not, one after the other.
You have got into the
tender hands,
I was suppressed
to the underneath.

You have got caressed by
all the hands; but,
I was just ignored by all others.

You have passed all the
milestones,
I sat on a cornerstone;
Watching you, since you born.
Sometimes, reaching you;
at a distance of a sigh.

Sometimes, atop,
the infinite blue sky.

One day I'll come close to you,
beside your bed,
and slowly to your body;
give up all your fears
and worries, I'll let you relax.

Let the others realize
that, I was with you always;
as I do with all the others.

Relax, close your eyes
Relax, and r.e..l…a…x.

The existence

To unload all the heaviness,
I spent the night, sitting alone
Under the roof of darkness.
Afar, the blinking little stars
Seemed like small holes
On a black umbrella.

The air was fresh and cool,
Fragrance of nature and
Handpicked little tea leaves
Roamed everywhere in
The chariot of silence.

In distance, unclear shadows
Of unknown trees chilled into
The grotto of mysteries
Spread by centuries
About the mountain town.

The darkness that surrounded,
Calloused with the music of nature.

Sitting alone in the porch
I was thinking
How do I approach?
The woes of my life in such
A way it may reach.

The night-birds sang in
Distance; calling their mates
To share some heat
By hugging with wings
Rubbing with beaks
They are asking
the meaning of loneliness.

Though nothing exists alone,
I would say, solitariness
Is the paradise of poets
But,
Alone, nothing exists.

The drama of life

Is it possible for life to be
completed without sorrow?
From the moment of one's birth;
till the heaviness of his (her)
last breath dissolves in his (her)
lungs, and exhales forever,
sorrow plays the inevitable role
in the drama of life.

It starts, when modern moms disagree
to feed their breast to the infant babies;
rather, they prefer to keep its
shape and beauty, that attract the opposite.
The first black shadow of sorrow falls there
in the face of an innocent baby.

When he (she) is being replanted from
the courtyards of happiness,

to the boundaries of classrooms,
where it starts to impose restrictions,
'no's, and forbids into the budding minds,
that causes to burn the wicks of sorrow
in their early ages.

At the end of teen, when their mates
separate from them, a bird of miseries
roosts in their oscillating minds.

Again, at the end of their joyous campus,
they are all becoming isolated weeping islands.
Their salty tears cause the oceans are being salted.
Then, when he (she) enters real life,
he (she) faces the reality of naked grief,
where, only his silhouettes would follow.

If the hero of the drama of life has
not played his (her) role, then the entire play
would have ended up with just an illusion.

Winter glimpses

The frozen wings of
Mediterranean winter
is all set to an encounter
with the last warrior
of surrendering summer.

After the fall of November
it is now December
my dear, I remember
the day, when you
came into my chamber
with the fragrance of the amber,
that was on the night of a December.

Pine trees stood lined,
like in a military drill, aligned.
Roads and roofs are covered
with the white blanket of nature.

Pine and cedar trees struggled
to hold the frozen snow rocks.
They looked as white pelicans
sheltered on the branches.

Silence, absolute silence;
tiny slices of blizzards
fluttered around us,
You and me, but
not two, (as we are now)
dived into the glittering world.

You did steal my heart
I have stolen your
concealed treasure.
Though it was chilled at night,
beneath the blanket,
we still could enjoy the warmth
of our special night;
that would always be
remembered in the
chillness of every December.

Wishes for tonight

Tonight, I wish that,
I could watch the stars
blinking in the far skies;
like a flock of fireflies
glittering above the rooftops
of absolute darkness.

Tonight, I wish that,
if I could stay on wet clouds
all the night, and wish to
purge the pain from my heart
as if we blow-off
trembling candlelight.

Tonight, I wish that,
if I could scream loudly by
standing in the middle of
the valley of silence

and to hear the echos reflects from
the surrounding mountains
of loneliness.
Tonight, I wish that
if I could oscillate in a swing that is
made of rain threads
and catch the shining moon
to brighten the face of my love
as it was her only condition for our love.

Tonight, I wish that
I could float in the air with her,
like a pappus flower,
and vanish in the clouds
Tonight and forever…

Preview

"Painting and poetry have one thing similar: they both spread colors and emotions. Here, both come from the heart of a person. Saleem Raza, the poet and an artist as well, spreads ensigns of emotions from his heart. The poet has knitted a tapestry of beautiful lines with intertwined emotions that inspired me to join in the journey throughout this book.

In the poem 'Beautiful is Night' it wonders me how the poet is seeing the things in the perspective of a blind couple? Every loss presupposes the absence of assured gain, which is well established in the poems, 'Victim of a Hellish Act' and 'Kindly Light', where Saleem effectively portrays love, support, care and protection.

'Love mostly happens in heaven, but sometimes on earth too.' These lines show Poet Saleem Raza's vision of his inner mind and give us a pure literary feast and pleasure in this little book of emotions. So we, the readers, would keep this beautiful collection of poetry as our personal and private pride."

– Sapana Anu George, Journalist and Columnist.

Thanks - To All My readers.

www.ingramcontent.com/pod-product-compliance
Lightning Source LLC
Chambersburg PA
CBHW021128130726
47988CB00003B/1210